AF270415

DETROIT
TIGERS

BY PATRICK DONNELLY

SportsZone

An Imprint of Abdo Publishing
abdobooks.com

abdobooks.com

Published by Abdo Publishing, a division of ABDO, PO Box 398166, Minneapolis, Minnesota 55439. Copyright © 2023 by Abdo Consulting Group, Inc. International copyrights reserved in all countries. No part of this book may be reproduced in any form without written permission from the publisher. SportsZone™ is a trademark and logo of Abdo Publishing.

Printed in the United States of America, North Mankato, Minnesota.
102022
012023

Cover Photo: Brian Rothmuller/Icon Sportswire/Getty Images
Interior Photos: Duane Burleson/Getty Images Sport/Getty Images, 4; Mark Rucker/Transcendental Graphics/Getty Images Sport/Getty Images, 7, 9; The Rucker Archive/Icon Sportswire, 10; Buyenlarge/Archive Photos/Getty Images, 12; AP Images, 14, 18, 22; George Rinhart/Corbis Historical/Getty Images, 16; Sporting News/Getty Images, 21; Focus on Sport/Getty Images, 24, 28, 31; Focus on Sport/Getty Images Sport/Getty Images, 27; Charles Bennett/AP Images, 32; Rich Pilling/MLB Photos/Getty Images Sport/Getty Images, 35; Bettmann/Getty Images, 36; Ronald Martinez/Getty Images Sport/Getty Images, 38; Mike Mulholland/Getty Images Sport/Getty Images, 41

Editor: Steph Giedd
Series Designer: Becky Daum

Library of Congress Control Number: 2022940475

Publisher's Cataloging-in-Publication Data

Names: Donnelly, Patrick, author.
Title: Detroit Tigers / by Patrick Donnelly
Description: Minneapolis, Minnesota: Abdo Publishing, 2023 | Series: Inside MLB | Includes online resources and index.
Identifiers: ISBN 9781098290177 (lib. bdg.) | ISBN 9781098275372 (ebook)
Subjects: LCSH: Detroit Tigers (Baseball team)--Juvenile literature. | Baseball teams--Juvenile literature. | Professional sports--Juvenile literature. | Sports franchises--Juvenile literature. | Major League Baseball (Organization)--Juvenile literature.
Classification: DDC 796.35764--dc23

CONTENTS

A HISTORY OF HITTERS

As Miguel Cabrera walked to the batter's box in the bottom of the first inning, he felt the pressure of history on his shoulders. The Detroit Tigers star was one hit away from 3,000 for his career. Only 32 other players had ever reached that milestone. On April 23, 2022, he was ready to join the club.

Cabrera had been stuck on 2,999 for a few days. He had gone hitless in five plate appearances. Then a rainout delayed his quest by another day. Finally, the Tigers and Colorado Rockies took the field on a perfect day for baseball—sunny, warm, no wind. More than 37,000 fans came out to Detroit's Comerica Park to witness history. Cabrera's mother, wife, and

Slugger Miguel Cabrera rips his 3,000th career hit, a single, on April 23, 2022, at Comerica Park in Detroit.

children were in the crowd too. The only problem was Cabrera's nerves. He later said he couldn't feel his legs during his first at-bat. That was just a sign of how much the moment meant to him.

With a runner on first and one out, Rockies pitcher Antonio Senzatela threw Cabrera two pitches on the outside part of the plate. Then he came inside with a fastball. But Cabrera was ready for it. He used his compact swing and strength to punch the ball through the right side of the infield for a base hit. He hadn't even left the batter's box before he raised his right index finger and pumped his fist in celebration.

Cabrera's teammates poured out of the dugout to congratulate him. The crowd gave him an extended ovation. He even got to hug his family during a brief ceremony behind home plate before the game resumed. Cabrera was just the third Tiger to join the 3,000-hit club. Sluggers Ty Cobb and Al Kaline were the other two. He also became the seventh player ever with 3,000 hits and 500 home runs. And to cap off a perfect day, the Tigers won 13–0.

COBB'S CATS

Cabrera is just the latest in a long line of outstanding hitters to have worn a Tigers uniform. The team's history dates back to 1901 with the founding of the American League (AL). It wasn't

No player in MLB history has a higher career batting average than former Tigers center fielder Ty Cobb, with .366.

long before one of the greatest hitters ever to play the game arrived in Detroit.

On August 30, 1905, an 18-year-old from Georgia named Ty Cobb made his debut as a center fielder with the Tigers. He batted fifth and got a base hit off future Hall of Famer Jack Chesbro. That hit was the first of 4,189 in his 24-year career. Cobb held the record for the most hits in Major League Baseball (MLB) history for 57 years. That historic record was not broken until 1985 by Pete Rose of the Cincinnati Reds.

Cobb was a fiery competitor who sometimes let his temper get the best of him. But his talent was undeniable. His .366 career batting average is a record that likely will never be broken. Cobb hit .400 three times and won 12 AL batting titles, including nine straight beginning in 1907.

That was also the year the Tigers won the first of three straight AL pennants. The 1907 Tigers were surprise contenders after winning just 71 games the year before. But in 1907, the 20-year-old Cobb gave the rest of the league a taste of what they could expect from him in the years to come. He not only hit .350 to lead the major leagues, he also drove in 119 runs and stole 53 bases.

Cobb had plenty of chances for runs batted in (RBIs) because he usually hit one spot behind fellow outfielder Sam Crawford in the Tigers' batting order. Crawford was a speedster

Tigers outfielder Sam Crawford hit an MLB-record 309 triples during his Hall of Fame career.

whose specialty was hitting triples. In that era, most ballparks were huge and featured large expanses of grass in the outfield. Crawford took advantage by driving the ball into the alleys between outfielders and letting his speed do the rest. More than 100 years later, he still held the MLB career record with 309 triples. And he led the league six times in that category.

The Tigers' first World Series ended in disappointment at Bennett Park in Detroit, as the team scored just one run in two losses after returning home to close out the series.

The Tigers were 7 1/2 games out of first place in mid-July. Then they caught fire, winning 15 of their next 18 games to take over the top spot in the AL standings. From there it was a three-team race to the finish, with the Chicago White Sox and Philadelphia Athletics challenging Detroit down the stretch. The situation looked bleak for the Tigers when they were swept in a doubleheader by the St. Louis Browns on September 14. But then they went on another run, winning 14 of 16 decisions with one tie. Detroit ended up 92–58 and edged the Athletics by 1 1/2 games.

HERE COME THE CUBS

That set up a World Series showdown with the Chicago Cubs. The National League (NL) champs were looking for revenge against the AL. The year before, the Cubs won a record 116 games in a 154-game season but lost to the White Sox in the World Series. The 1907 Cubs won 107 games on the strength of their pitching—their team earned-run average (ERA) of 1.73 remains the lowest ever posted over an entire season.

The Tigers proved to be no match for the Cubs' aces. Game 1 was called due to darkness. The teams were tied 3–3 after 12 innings. In the next four games, the Tigers scored three runs total. The Cubs rolled to four straight wins and their first World Series title.

The next year was more of the same. This time, the Tigers won the AL by half a game over Cleveland, with the White Sox just a game and a half out. Cobb hit .324 and led the league in hits, doubles, triples, RBIs, and batting average. Crawford hit 16 triples and led the league in homers with seven. And the Tigers ran into the Cubs in the World Series again.

Tigers pitcher George Mullin led the AL in win/loss percentage (.784) and led the majors with 29 wins during the 1909 season.

Chicago was still powered by its pitchers, with a team ERA of 2.14. Detroit actually fared better at the plate than it had the year before. In Game 1, the Tigers registered 10 hits in a 10–6 loss. And they took the third game 8–3, with Cobb collecting three singles and a double. But they scored just one run total in the other three games, including two shutout losses at home in the final two games of the series.

The 1909 Tigers had the best shot at winning the World Series. And they came closest of the three pennant-winning teams. Cobb won the Triple Crown that year, leading the majors with a .377 batting average, nine home runs, and 107 RBIs. Right-hander George Mullin went 29–8, while Ed Willett won 21 games as the Tigers went 98–84 overall.

The Cubs won 104 games that year. But they lost the NL pennant to the Pittsburgh Pirates, who posted an amazing 110–42 record. At the time, there were no playoffs, with only the league champions advancing to the World Series. The World Series came down to Game 7 in Detroit. And the home team fell apart. The Tigers committed three errors and couldn't put together a rally against Pirates ace Babe Adams. The 8–0 loss marked the end of Detroit's three-year rule over the AL.

Crawford and Cobb continued their assault on AL pitching over the next few years. Crawford led the league in triples four more times and won three RBI titles before ending his MLB career after the 1917 season. Cobb hit a career-high .419 in 1911 and set a modern era (post-1900) record with 96 stolen bases in 1915. But the team didn't finish higher than second place over the next two decades. Cobb took over as player-manager from 1921 to 1926. He then played two years with the Philadelphia Athletics before retiring at age 41.

As the 1930s dawned, the Tigers were just hoping to break into the top half of the league. Instead, they found themselves at the top of the baseball world.

HARRY HEILMANN

Right fielder Harry Heilmann was a rare bright spot on the dreary Tigers teams of the 1910s and 1920s. He filled Sam Crawford's role as Ty Cobb's top sidekick, proving to be one of the greatest right-handed hitters of his era. Heilmann won four batting titles, hitting at least .393 in each of those seasons. Even 100 years later, his career average of .342 ranked seventh all-time among modern MLB players.

THE SWINGING THIRTIES

n the early 1930s, the Tigers began assembling a talented group of players who would turn them into pennant contenders. They already had second baseman Charlie Gehringer, who cracked the starting lineup in 1926. In 1933 22-year-old first baseman Hank Greenberg joined the club. And in the months before the 1934 season began, the Tigers traded for catcher Mickey Cochrane and outfielder Goose Goslin. All four would go on to the Baseball Hall of Fame. And all four would play key roles as the Tigers clawed their way to the top of the AL standings.

Baseball had become a hitter's game in the late 1920s, and by 1934 the Tigers were well-equipped to join in the

Tigers second baseman Charlie Gehringer led the league in several offensive categories in 1929 including hits (215), doubles (45), triples (19), and stolen bases (27).

After winning the 1928 AL MVP with the Athletics, Hall of Fame catcher Mickey Cochrane won another in 1934 with the Tigers.

offensive fireworks. Gehringer batted .356 with a career-high 127 RBIs. Greenberg led the majors with 63 doubles and chipped in 139 RBIs along with a .339 batting average. Goslin hit .305 and drove in 100 runs.

As for Cochrane, he pulled double duty as the Detroit catcher and manager. He came over from the Philadelphia Athletics. There he had won two World Series with the Athletics and earned a reputation as a fierce, inspirational leader. "He was the greatest fighting spirit on the ball field," Greenberg noted. "He'd go through a brick wall to catch a ball."

Cochrane was named the AL Most Valuable Player (MVP) in 1934, though not so much for his statistics as for his overall impact on the Tigers. He hit a respectable .320 with 75 RBIs. And his performance, along with that of his teammates, helped turn the Tigers into an offensive force. Their team batting average jumped from .269 to .300 in his first year in Detroit.

The Tigers led the majors in hits, doubles, and stolen bases on the way to averaging an eye-popping 6.2 runs scored per game.

The Tigers had decent pitching as well. They finished second in the AL in ERA and strikeouts. Their ace, 24-year-old Schoolboy Rowe, went 24–8 and won 16 straight games between June 15 and August 25. Tommy Bridges won 22 games, while Firpo Marberry and Elden Auker were effective as starters and out of the bullpen.

A TENSE WORLD SERIES

Detroit went 101–53 and won the AL pennant by seven games over the New York Yankees. In the World Series, the Tigers faced the St. Louis Cardinals. The NL champs had a style of play similar to that of the Tigers. They hit the ball all over the park and had enough pitching to survive the heavy-hitting lineups common in that era.

The teams split the first two games in Detroit. The Tigers started Game 1 with veteran General Crowder on the mound. He had gone 5–1 down the stretch after the Tigers picked him up from the Washington Senators in August. But the Cardinals stung Crowder for four runs and added four more off Marberry in an 8–3 victory. Game 2 went 12 innings, with Rowe pitching a complete game for Detroit. Goslin's single in the 12th scored

Gehringer from second for a 3–2 win that evened the series at a game apiece.

Game 3 in St. Louis was another pitchers' duel, with Paul Dean shutting down the Tigers in a 4–1 Cardinals victory. Detroit responded with 13 hits in a 10–4 victory to even the series once again. Bridges was brilliant in Game 5, holding St. Louis to seven hits in a 3–1 win. That sent the series back to

Detroit with the Tigers needing just one more win for their first World Series title. But the Cardinals wouldn't go down easily. Dean's RBI single off Rowe in the seventh inning gave St. Louis a 4–3 victory in Game 6.

Game 7 was played in front of nearly 41,000 Tigers fans at Detroit's Navin Field. The Cardinals quickly put the Tigers in a bad mood with a seven-run third inning. The bad news continued for the Tigers. Cardinals pitcher Dizzy Dean, who was Paul Dean's brother, tossed a six-hit shutout as the Cardinals took the series with an 11–0 rout.

BOUNCING BACK

The Tigers had lost four straight World Series. But they were determined to end that streak in 1935. They put up big offensive numbers again, averaging 6.0 runs per game. Greenberg led the majors with 36 homers and 168 RBIs. Gehringer and Goslin each drove in 100 runs as well.

MOTOR CITY MADNESS

Game 7 of the 1934 World Series was stained by an incident in the sixth inning as Ducky Medwick of the Cardinals slid hard into third base, clipping the Tigers' Marv Owen. The two players almost started a fight. When Medwick went to his spot in left field in the bottom half of the inning, Tigers fans pelted him with whatever they could find—bottles, fruit, scorecards. Medwick had to be replaced before the game could continue.

And Detroit again had just enough pitching to carry the team to the pennant.

The Tigers' 93–58 record left them three games ahead of the Yankees at the end of the season. That brought a World Series rematch against the Chicago Cubs. Though their most recent matchup had been 27 years earlier, Tigers fans still cringed at the thought of the Cubs dominating their club in back-to-back World Series. This time, the 100-win Cubs came into the World Series red-hot. They had won 21 straight games to clinch the NL pennant on the season's final weekend. But the Cubs would have their hands full with the hard-hitting Tigers.

Once again, the Tigers lost Game 1 at home, but they rebounded quickly. They began the first inning of Game 2 with four straight hits, capped by Greenberg's two-run homer that gave them a quick 4–0 lead. From there, Bridges did the rest as the Tigers cruised to an 8–3 victory. The only drawback was Greenberg suffering a broken wrist on a slide at home plate. He would miss the rest of the series.

In Game 3, the Tigers rallied for four runs in the eighth to take a 5–3 lead, only to see the Cubs score twice in the ninth to tie the game. In the 11th, Detroit center fielder Jo-Jo White's two-out single scored Marv Owen from second to give the Tigers a 6–5 lead. Then Rowe closed it out, striking out the last two Cubs hitters to seal the win.

First baseman Hank Greenberg led the AL in home runs in four of his 12 seasons with the Tigers. He also led the league in RBIs in four seasons.

Detroit took a 3–1 lead in the series as Crowder—the pitcher who was charged with the loss for Game 1 a year earlier—pitched a five-hitter in a 2–1 victory. With a chance to clinch the series in Chicago, the Tigers came up short in a 3–1 Cubs win. However, back in Detroit, the Tigers came through in the clutch.

With the game tied 3–3, Chicago's Stan Hack led off the top of the ninth with a triple. But Bridges retired the next three batters without allowing Hack to advance. In the bottom of the ninth, Cochrane hit a one-out single, moved to second on a ground-out, and scored on a single by Goslin. At long last, the Detroit Tigers had their first World Series title.

Pitcher General Crowder played his final three MLB seasons with Detroit, retiring after the 1936 season.

The Tigers made it back to the Fall Classic twice in the following decade. Greenberg was named the AL MVP in 1940. However, Detroit fell to the Cincinnati Reds in a seven-game World Series. Greenberg left the team in 1942 to serve in the armed forces. But he returned midway through the 1945 season. In his first game in 3 1/2 years, Greenberg homered, to the delight of 48,000 fans who welcomed him back to Tiger Stadium. Future Hall of Famer Hal Newhouser won 25 games and his second straight AL MVP Award. Greenberg's ninth-inning grand slam on the last day of the season helped secure the pennant for the Tigers.

In the World Series, Detroit faced the Cubs. This World Series went to seven Games, but it has been described as one of the worst ever played. There were several mental mistakes by the veterans of both teams. Newhouser got rocked in Game 1, resulting in a 9–0 Cubs victory. The Tigers bounced back, as Greenberg's three-run homer solidified a 4–1 win in Game 2. The series was tied 2–2 when Greenberg struck again. This time he hit three doubles to back Newhouser in an 8–4 win. The Cubs took Game 6 in extra innings, thanks to Hank Borowy's relief efforts. But they failed to carry over any momentum to the next game. Just two days later, Borowy's arm was exhausted going into Game 7. As a result, he allowed base hits to the first three batters before being removed. The Tigers hit for five runs in the top of the first and cruised to a 9–3 win, giving Detroit its second title. The Tigers won despite having a .223 batting average. Greenberg was the hero of the World Series on offense for the Tigers, though, smacking three doubles, hitting in seven runs, and reaching base 13 times.

The Tigers soon hit another dry spell and spent most of the 1950s near the bottom of the standings. But it wouldn't be long before October baseball returned to Motor City.

LIGHTNING STRIKES TWICE

Tigers pitcher Virgil Trucks had one of the stranger seasons on record in 1952. The 35-year-old right-hander finished the year with a 5–19 record. But two of his victories were no-hitters. On May 15 in Detroit, he struck out seven and walked just one in a 1–0 win over the Washington Senators. Then on August 25, he struck out eight and walked one as he no-hit the New York Yankees 1–0. He was just the third pitcher in MLB history to throw two no-hitters in a season.

CHAPTER 3

YEAR OF THE TIGER

The race for the AL pennant in 1967 was one for the history books. On September 7, with just over three weeks left in the season, four teams were tied for first place. The Tigers, Minnesota Twins, Chicago White Sox, and Boston Red Sox spent the rest of the month bouncing back and forth at the top. As of September 6, each team spent at least one day in first place. And it took until the final day of the season for Boston to clinch the pennant, with Detroit and Minnesota finishing one game out.

Still, all was not lost for the Tigers. The grit and fight they showed in that tight race carried over to the next season. Manager Mayo Smith, in his first year in Detroit, learned which

Tigers pitcher Denny McLain was a two-time Cy Young Award winner in 1968 and 1969.

buttons to push to get the best out of his players. And his young players, many of whom were still in their mid-20s, had gained important big-league experience.

Historians now refer to 1968 as the Year of the Pitcher. MLB had increased the size of the strike zone in 1963. And throughout the decade, pitchers increasingly dominated hitters. The trend reached its peak in 1968, when the average ERA in the AL was 2.98 and the hitters combined for a .230 batting average, the lowest in history.

Fortunately for the Tigers, they thrived in the Year of the Pitcher. That's because they had two excellent ones. Their ace was right-hander Denny McLain. The 24-year-old, who was already a 20-game winner in the majors, made history that year. He was the first pitcher in 34 years to win at least 30 games in a season. McLain's 31–6 record and 1.96 ERA made him a lock for the AL Cy Young Award, awarded to the best pitcher in the league. He was also named the league MVP, which is rare for pitchers.

Meanwhile, lefty Mickey Lolich had averaged 15 wins per season over the previous four years. He also led the majors with six shutouts in 1967. He would prove to be one of the Tigers' most reliable players in their biggest moments to come.

Their lineup was balanced between veterans and youngsters. Future Hall of Famer Al Kaline was a 13-time

Tigers pitcher Mickey Lolich earned wins in all three games he started during the 1968 World Series. For his efforts, he was named the World Series MVP.

All-Star and had been the face of the team for over a decade. On May 19, 1968, Kaline broke Hank Greenberg's team record with his 307th career home run. But a week later, he was hit by a pitch and suffered a fracture in his forearm. He missed six weeks, and when he returned, Smith rotated him between right field, left field, and first base.

Hall of Fame slugger Al Kaline gets a hit against the St. Louis Cardinals in the 1968 World Series.

That rotation was necessary because in Kaline's absence, a trio of young outfielders proved to be worthy of starting spots as well. Left fielder Willie Horton slammed 36 homers and hit .285. Center fielder Mickey Stanley won a Gold Glove Award as one of the three best fielding outfielders in the league. He was also a fixture near the top of the batting order. Right fielder Jim Northrop led the team in doubles and RBIs. Meanwhile, first baseman Norm Cash and tough-as-nails catcher Bill Freehan each hit 25 homers.

BRING ON THE CARDINALS

The Tigers won 103 games and cruised to the pennant. But before the World Series against the St. Louis Cardinals, Smith had a tough decision to make. He wanted to get all four of his outfielders and Cash into the lineup. Smith found a unique solution. In the final week of the season, with the pennant already clinched, he moved Stanley to shortstop to replace light-hitting Ray Oyler. Stanley had never played shortstop in the majors. The move could have easily backfired on Smith. But he had faith the athletic Stanley would get the job done.

The Tigers defense had to be strong. This is because the offense wasn't expected to do much against the Cardinals, especially when ace Bob Gibson was on the mound. Gibson was even more dominant in the NL than McLain was in the AL. The flamethrowing right-hander went 22–9 with 13 shutouts and a 1.12 ERA. Like McLain, he pulled the Cy Young–MVP double in the NL. And the two aces were set to face each other in Game 1.

It turned out to be no match. Gibson set a World Series record with 17 strikeouts. McLain, battling a sore shoulder, lasted just five innings as the Cardinals won 4–0. Lolich was the star in Game 2, holding the Cards to one run and hitting a home run—the only one of his career—as the Tigers rolled to an 8–1 victory.

But back in Detroit, the Cardinals took the next two and threatened to run away with the title. Lolich came up big again, going the distance as the Tigers rallied to win Game 5. But the Cardinals had two chances at home to win the World Series. Game 6 quickly became a blowout. The Tigers scored 12 runs through the first three innings, giving McLain all the support he needed.

The Cardinals still had to be confident with Gibson in line to start Game 7. But Lolich stole the show. He held St. Louis to just five hits. Meanwhile the Tigers finally reached the St. Louis ace for three runs in the seventh to win 4–1. Lolich was the series MVP with his three complete-game victories. And the Tigers had their first title since 1935.

McLain won his second straight Cy Young Award in 1969. All those innings caught up with him, though, and his career was derailed by arm trouble.

THE BIRD

Tigers rookie Mark "the Bird" Fidrych took the league by storm in 1976. The 21-year-old right-hander went 19–9 with a 2.34 ERA. But his popularity stemmed more from his quirky personality. He talked to the ball, groomed the mound with his bare hands, and generally seemed to be enjoying himself when he pitched. Tall and lanky with long, curly hair, Fidrych resembled the Sesame Street character that gave him his nickname. In his second season, Fidrych developed arm troubles that ended up cutting his career short. But fans in Detroit still remember 1976 as the Summer of the Bird.

However, the core of that championship team was still together when the Tigers won the AL East title in 1972. Lolich, now the undeniable leader of the pitching staff, won 22 games, while right-hander Joe Coleman went 19–14.

Tigers catcher Bill Freehan (11) catches an excited Mickey Lolich as their team celebrates Detroit's third World Series title as a franchise in 1968.

Unfortunately, the Tigers ran into a powerhouse Oakland Athletics team that would win the next three World Series. Detroit gave the A's all they could handle in the AL Championship Series (ALCS), which baseball had added in 1969 to expand the postseason. But Oakland advanced with a 2–1 win in Game 5 at Tiger Stadium.

After that, the Tigers roster began to turn over due to retirements and free agency. But by the end of the decade, the core of one of the greatest teams in MLB history was beginning to form in Detroit.

CHAPTER 4

MOTOR CITY MAGIC

Detroit pitcher Jack Morris threw his nastiest slider. Chicago White Sox slugger Ron Kittle couldn't check his swing in time. The Detroit ace's eighth strikeout of the game sealed a 4–0 victory. Catcher Lance Parrish leaped into Morris's arms as their teammates poured onto the field to celebrate. Morris had just completed the Tigers' first no-hitter in more than 25 years. They hadn't clinched the 1984 pennant—it was only April 7—but in many ways, that chilly afternoon in Chicago served notice to the rest of the AL. The Tigers were going to be tough to beat.

Morris's no-hitter was just part of an incredible season that started with a historic streak. The Tigers won their first

Tigers ace Jack Morris celebrates after throwing the final pitch in a no-hitter against the Chicago White Sox in 1984. He led the AL in strikeouts (232) the previous season.

nine games that year. Then, after losing one, they won their next seven. Their 16–1 start gave the Tigers a six-game lead in the AL East. But they were far from done. A week later, they launched another 16–1 run that put their record at 35–5. It was the best record any MLB team had ever posted through 40 games. The rest of the division never had a chance.

The 1984 Tigers weren't loaded with star power. But they were at least solid across every position on the field. And they were especially strong up the middle. Parrish hit 33 homers and threw out 46 percent of opposing base stealers. Second baseman Lou Whitaker and shortstop Alan Trammell were the best double-play combo in the game. And slugging center fielder Chet Lemon had speed and a cannon arm. All four were All-Stars that year, as were Morris and closer Willie Hernández.

The most important player on that team, however, might have been right fielder Kirk Gibson. The Michigan native had been a college football star, but he loved baseball too. In 1984 Gibson was 27 years old and in his athletic prime. His rare combination of speed and power were on display all season. He led the team with 10 triples and 29 stolen bases. Gibson was also second to Parrish with 27 home runs and 91 RBIs.

The pitching staff included three right-handers—Morris, Dan Petry, and Milt Wilcox—who each won at least 17 games. The bullpen was just as strong. Hernández saved 32 games

in 33 chances and won nine more. Under manager Sparky Anderson, Hernández worked more than the typical closer—he made 80 appearances and pitched 140 1/3 innings that year. He ended up winning the AL Cy Young and MVP awards for his efforts.

After their historic start, the Tigers were never seriously threatened. They led the East by 10 games at the end of June. And they coasted from there, finishing 104–58, 15 games ahead of the Toronto Blue Jays. The postseason brought more of the same. Detroit swept the Kansas City Royals in the ALCS. And the San Diego Padres were no match in the World Series, falling

Detroit slugger Kirk Gibson celebrates after hitting his first of two home runs in Game 5 of the 1984 World Series.

to the Tigers in five games. Morris won both of his starts. And Gibson's three-run homer in the eighth inning of Game 5 put a fitting capper on the series. Hernández got the final three outs, and Tiger Stadium erupted. Fans poured onto the field to mob the players gathered on the infield. Fans set off fireworks outside the ballpark while others tore up hunks of turf from the Tiger Stadium field as souvenirs. The players quickly rushed into the safety of the clubhouse to continue celebrating a truly remarkable season.

ONE AND DONE

That Tigers team felt like a dynasty in the making. But they never returned to the World Series. After two back-to-back third-place finishes, Detroit won another division title in 1987. But the Tigers were upset by the Minnesota Twins in the ALCS. Two years later, the bottom fell out, as Detroit lost 103 games. It was the team's worst season since 1952.

Unfortunately for Tigers fans, that was a sign of bad things to come. After a second-place finish in 1991, the Tigers ended the year no closer than 10 games back for the next 14 seasons. That stretch included some incredibly dark times. Detroit lost 109 games in 1996. The Tigers lost 106 games in 2002 and then fell to 43–119 in 2003. That was

ALMOST PERFECT

Right-hander Armando Galarraga pitched a perfect game for the Tigers. But it doesn't appear in the record books. Galarraga retired the first 26 Cleveland batters he faced on June 2, 2010. Then, with two outs in the ninth, first baseman Miguel Cabrera fielded a ground ball and flipped it to Galarraga covering the base. Umpire Jim Joyce ruled the runner safe, though replays showed he was out. Galarraga retired the next batter but officially had to settle for a one-hit shutout. Joyce later apologized, and Galarraga accepted, saying, "Nobody's perfect."

 Tigers shortstop Carlos Guillén played eight of his 14 MLB seasons with Detroit, ending in 2011.

the worst record of any team since the first-year New York Mets
went 40–120 in 1962.

ON THE REBOUND

In 2004, however, the Tigers posted the second-biggest
turnaround in AL history. The addition of veteran catcher Iván
Rodríguez and shortstop Carlos Guillén helped Detroit win
29 more games that year. And just two years later, the Tigers
shocked the baseball world by making a run all the way to the
World Series. Guillén and Rodríguez were the team's only .300
hitters. But the lineup was balanced, with four players hitting
at least 24 homers and no starter hitting worse than .253.

Two starting pitchers at the opposite stages of their
careers turned in strong seasons as well. Lefty Kenny Rogers,
who signed as a free agent in the offseason, went 17–8 and
earned his third straight All-Star berth at age 41. Meanwhile,
23-year-old Justin Verlander was named the AL Rookie of the
Year after winning 17 games. The Tigers went 95–67, then
knocked off the New York Yankees and Oakland Athletics in the
AL playoffs. However, they fell to the St. Louis Cardinals in five
games in the World Series.

After the 2007 season, the Tigers traded for first baseman
Miguel Cabrera. The Venezuelan slugger led the AL with 37
homers his first season in Detroit. He went on to win four

OLD ENGLISH D

batting titles and two AL MVP Awards, one of which was in his amazing 2012 season. That year, he was the first Triple Crown winner in 45 years, leading the league with 44 homers, 139 RBIs, and a .330 batting average. No one else has accomplished that feat since.

Verlander emerged as one of the game's best pitchers, earning the Cy Young and MVP awards in 2011 when he led the majors with 24 wins and 250 strikeouts. He was joined in the rotation by fellow right-hander Max Scherzer, the AL Cy Young winner in 2013 when he went 21–3. The deadly one-two punch led the Tigers to four straight AL Central titles starting in 2011. However, only once did they advance to the World Series. That was in 2012, when they were swept by the San Francisco Giants.

When Verlander and Scherzer moved on, the Tigers once again slipped to the bottom of the standings. But Cabrera continued to give fans a reason to show up to Comerica Park, and the team began rebuilding. Starter Tarik Skubal and closer Gregory Soto emerged as potential All-Stars on the mound,

Tigers designated hitter Miguel Cabrera rips an RBI double against the Baltimore Orioles at Comerica Park in Detroit during the 2022 season.

while first baseman Spencer Torkelson and center fielder Willi Castro were building blocks in the lineup. The addition of free agent shortstop Javy Báez in 2022 gave fans reason to hope winning baseball would return to Motor City.

TIMELINE

1901

The Detroit Tigers begin play as a member of the AL.

1905

Ty Cobb debuts for the Tigers.

1909

Detroit wins its third straight AL pennant but loses in the World Series for the third straight year.

1926

Cobb plays his final season in Detroit before finishing his Hall of Fame career in Philadelphia with the Athletics.

1934

The Tigers win the AL pennant but lose to the St. Louis Cardinals in seven games in the World Series.

1935

Detroit finally wins its first World Series, defeating the Chicago Cubs in six games.

1940

The Tigers win the pennant for the sixth time but lose the World Series to the Cincinnati Reds in seven games.

1945

Hank Greenberg returns from military service to lead Detroit to the pennant and a World Series victory over the Cubs.

1968

Thanks to Denny McLain's and Mickey Lolich's efforts, the Tigers finish the Year of the Pitcher as World Series champions over the Cardinals in seven games.

1972

The Tigers win their first AL East title before falling to the Oakland Athletics in the ALCS.

1976

Mark "the Bird" Fidrych becomes a national sensation as he wins the AL Rookie of the Year award.

1984

The Tigers start the season 35–5 and roll to the World Series title, losing just one game in the postseason.

2003

The Tigers set an AL record by losing 119 games.

2006

Just three years after their disastrous season, the Tigers reach the World Series, falling to the Cardinals in five games.

2010

Right-hander Armando Galarraga pitches a perfect game for the Tigers. But an admittedly flubbed call by the umpire on the final out keeps it out of the record books.

2011

Justin Verlander wins the AL Cy Young and MVP awards as he leads the Tigers to the first of four straight division titles.

2012

The Tigers return to the World Series but are swept by the San Francisco Giants.

2022

Miguel Cabrera becomes the 33rd player to register 3,000 career hits with a single against the Colorado Rockies on April 23.

TEAM FACTS

FRANCHISE HISTORY

Detroit Tigers (1901–)

WORLD SERIES CHAMPIONSHIPS

1935, 1945, 1968, 1984

KEY PLAYERS

Miguel Cabrera (2008–)
Ty Cobb (1905–26)
Sam Crawford (1903–17)
Bill Freehan (1961, 1963–76)
Charlie Gehringer (1924–42)
Hank Greenberg (1930,
   1933–41, 1945–47)
Al Kaline (1953–74)
Mickey Lolich (1963–75)
Jack Morris (1977–90)
Alan Trammell (1977–96)
Justin Verlander (2005–17)
Lou Whitaker (1977–95)

KEY MANAGERS

Sparky Anderson (1979–95)
Hughie Jennings (1907–20)
Jim Leyland (2006–13)

HOME STADIUMS

Bennett Park (1901–11)
Tiger Stadium (1912–99)
   Also known as:
   Navin Field (1912–37)
   Briggs Stadium (1938–60)
Comerica Park (2000–)

CIRCLE THE BASES

On May 5, 1925, Ty Cobb collected 16 total bases (three home runs, a double, and two singles) in a 14–8 win over the St. Louis Browns. That set a single-game AL record.

DOUBLE TROUBLE

Since MLB established the Cy Young Award in 1956, seven AL pitchers have won both the Cy Young and MVP awards in the same season. Three of them played for the Tigers—Denny McLain in 1968, Willie Hernández in 1984, and Justin Verlander in 2011.

STAYING PUT

The Tigers, Cleveland Guardians, Boston Red Sox, and the Chicago White Sox are the only four AL teams still playing in the same city as they did in 1901 when the AL was founded.

SPARKLING PERFORMANCE

Sparky Anderson is the first manager to win 100 games and a World Series in both leagues. His Cincinnati Reds won 100 games three times and won two World Series in the 1970s. Then he led the Tigers to 104 wins and a World Series title in 1984.

GLOSSARY

ace
A team's best starting pitcher.

berth
A spot in a competition or tournament earned through previous results.

bullpen
The area of a baseball field where relief pitchers warm up; also used to refer to a team's relievers as a group.

closer
A pitcher who comes in at the end of the game to secure a win for his team.

dynasty
A team that has an extended period of success, usually winning multiple championships in the process.

free agent
A player whose rights are not owned by any team.

no-hitter
A complete game in which a team does not allow any hits.

pennant
Another name for a league championship; in MLB, refers to winning either the American or National League.

perfect game
A complete game in which a team does not allow any batter to reach base.

rookie
A professional athlete in his or her first year of competition.

shutout
A complete game in which a team allows no runs.

veteran
A player who has played for many years.

MORE INFORMATION

BOOKS

Flynn, Brendan. *The MLB Encyclopedia*. Minneapolis, MN: Abdo Publishing, 2022.

Gitlin, Marty. *MLB*. Minneapolis, MN: Abdo Publishing, 2021.

Hewson, Anthony K. *GOATs of Baseball*. Minneapolis, MN: Abdo Publishing, 2022.

ONLINE RESOURCES

To learn more about the Detroit Tigers, please visit **abdobooklinks.com** or scan this QR code. These links are routinely monitored and updated to provide the most current information available.

INDEX

ABOUT THE AUTHOR

Patrick Donnelly is a freelance writer who lives in Minneapolis, Minnesota. He has covered Major League Baseball for more than 20 years.